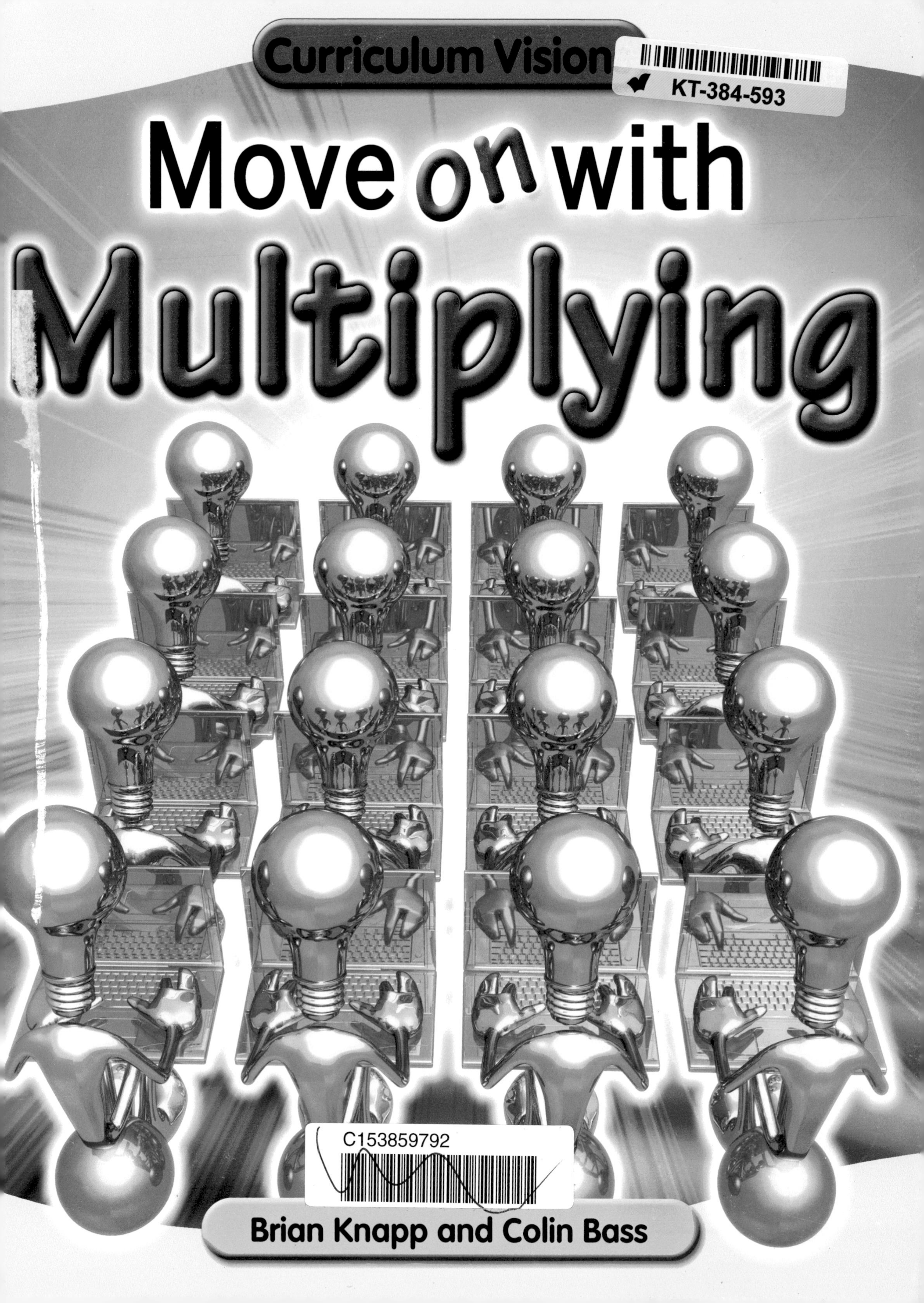
Curriculum Visions
Move on with
Multiplying
Brian Knapp and Colin Bass

A CVP Book

Series Concept
Brian Knapp, BSc, PhD

Text contributed by
Brian Knapp, BSc, PhD, and Colin Bass, BSc, MA

Editors
Lorna Gilbert, Barbara Carragher, and Gillian Gatehouse

Senior Designer
Adele Humphries, BA, PGCE

Illustrations
David Woodroffe

Designed and produced by
Atlantic Europe Publishing

Printed in China by
WKT Company Ltd

Curriculum Visions Move on with Maths – Multiplying
A CIP record for this book is available from the British Library

ISBN: 978 1 86214 557 3

Picture credits
All photographs are from the Earthscape Picture Library and ShutterStock collections.

This product is manufactured from sustainable managed forests. For every tree cut down at least one more is planted.

Look out for these sections to help you learn more about each topic:

Remember... This provides a summary of the key concept(s) on each two-page entry. Use it to revise what you have learned.

Can you do this? These problems reinforce the concepts learned on a particular spread, and can be used to test existing knowledge.

Answers to the problems set in the 'Move on with Maths' series can be found at: **www.curriculumvisions.com/moveOnAnswers**

Place value

To make it easy for you to see exactly what we are doing, you will find coloured columns behind the numbers in all the examples on this and the following pages. This is what the colours mean:

Ten thousands of units	Thousands of units	Hundreds of units	Tens of units	Units		Tenths of a unit	Hundredths of a unit	Thousandths of a unit
10,000	1,000	100	10	1		$\frac{1}{10}$	$\frac{1}{100}$	$\frac{1}{1,000}$
7	1	9	6	4	.	2	3	5

Whole numbers — Decimal point — Decimal parts

Contents

Why multiply?

Multiplying is the same as adding the same numbers over and over again. You multiply to save time.

Adding many of the same thing is very common. For example, you may go into a shop and ask for six cartons of milk or eight snack bars. You could write out a list and start adding each item, but you don't have to. Instead, you multiply.

Here are examples of the kind of problem that multiplication makes easy, although you won't find out how easy until you turn to the next page...

Jordan had already earned **£5** a week for four weeks by delivering free newspapers. The money was building up. He reckoned he would not need to spend it all, so he opened a savings account. He decided to save **£3** a week. How much could he put into the new account from the money he had already earned?

Week 1	**£3**	
Weeks 1 & 2	**£3 + £3**	**= £6**
Weeks 1, 2 & 3	**£3 + £3 + £3**	**= £6 + £3 = £9**
Weeks 1, 2, 3 & 4	**£3 + £3 + £3 + £3**	**= £9 + £3 = £12**

Jordan would also get interest on this **£12** and on any more he chose to save. By the way, savings mount up. Keeping money in a savings account like this is a very sensible thing to do and much better than keeping cash at home.

Lisa goes shopping

Lisa's family were having three guests for the week. Each insisted on having a boiled egg for their breakfast. So they needed **3** eggs for each of **7** days. So Lisa had to work out how many eggs to buy.

+ + = **3 eggs each day**

Lisa began by drawing out **3** eggs on a sheet of paper, grouping them in lines for each day of the week. Then she added the daily totals.

	Aunt Effy		Aunt Freda		Uncle Seamus		
Day 1		+		+		=	**3**
Day 2		+		+		=	**3**
Day 3		+		+		=	**3**
Day 4		+		+		=	**3**
Day 5		+		+		=	**3**
Day 6		+		+		=	**3**
Day 7		+		+		=	**3**
Total number of eggs required							**21**

By adding, Lisa found that it took a long time to discover that she needed **21** eggs.

But this is a very slow way of working things out. This is why we use multiplication. To find out how, turn the page.

Remember... It is often possible to draw a picture when you don't know how to do a calculation. Once you can see the drawing, you can often see how to work it out.

Can you do this? Can you find how many eggs there are in the photograph above without counting every one of them?

How to multiply

The key to multiplying is to count rows and columns.

Counting rows and columns

Lisa's drawing arranged the eggs into **7** rows each containing **3** eggs; that is, she had **7** rows and **3** columns. So Lisa actually needed **7** lots of **3**.

We already know that the total is **21** eggs. We can first write this down just as we might say it in conversation as:

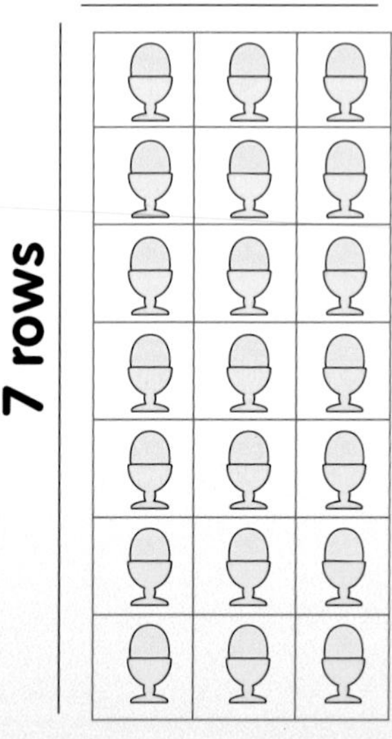

7 lots of 3 makes 21

Now change the words 'lots of' to 'multiplied by' and 'makes' to 'equals':

7 multiplied by 3 equals 21

Finally, we get the number equation:

$$7 \times 3 = 21$$

Smart work

Lisa was just going out to buy **21** eggs when she found another uncle was coming to stay, so Lisa was going to need more eggs.

But Lisa was too smart to start counting from the beginning again because she already knew that **7 × 3 = 21**.

One extra person would need one egg for each day of the week, or **7** eggs, so the total was:

$$21 + 7 = 28$$

Which she could also write down as:

$$7 + 7 + 7 + 7 = 28$$

but faster still as:

$$7 \times 4 = 28$$

As you can see, the more adding there is to do, the more useful multiplication is!

21

7

Conrad enjoys watching American football on satellite TV. Jacksonville Jaguars are leading Pittsburgh Steelers by **20** points to **6**. Steelers cannot rely on conversions. They have not been good at scoring them lately. If Jaguars do not score again, how many touchdowns do Steelers need to take the lead?

A touchdown is worth six points. On page 23 of *Curriculum Visions Move on with maths: Adding*, there is an adding square for sixes, in case you need to count in half-dozens. Using it, you can answer Conrad's question.

2 x 6 = 6 + 6 = 12

3 x 6 = 12 + 6 = 18

4 x 6 = 18 + 6 = 24 and so on.

These are **multiplying facts**. It is useful to learn them.

As Jaguars lead by **20 – 6 = 14** points, **12** points will not be enough for Steelers, so they need **18**.

18 = 3 x 6, so Steelers need **3** touchdowns.

Nancy wanted to read a fashion magazine regularly. She agreed to pay her Mum **£2** a week towards the household magazine bill. She has fallen **8** weeks behind in her payments. How much does she owe?

Week	**1**	**2**	**3**	**4**	**5**	**6**	**7**	**8**
Debt	**2**	**4**	**6**	**8**	**10**	**12**	**14**	**16**

So **8 x 2 = 16**. Nancy owes **£16**, which will make a big hole in her savings. This shows that it is wise to pay off any debt as quickly as possible and not let it build up. It is better to have no debt at all.

Remember... Multiplication saves time. For example, **3 + 3 + 3 + 3**. There are **4** of the same number in this list, so we can write it as **4 × 3**.

Can you do this? Can you use something on these pages to work out how many days there are in three weeks?

Multiply in any order

You can multiply numbers in any order.

Mandy and car washing

Mandy had been told by a friend that she would make more money by saving **£3** for **4** weeks at car washing than by saving **£4** for **3** weeks. To find out if this was true, she put together a block of **12** squares.

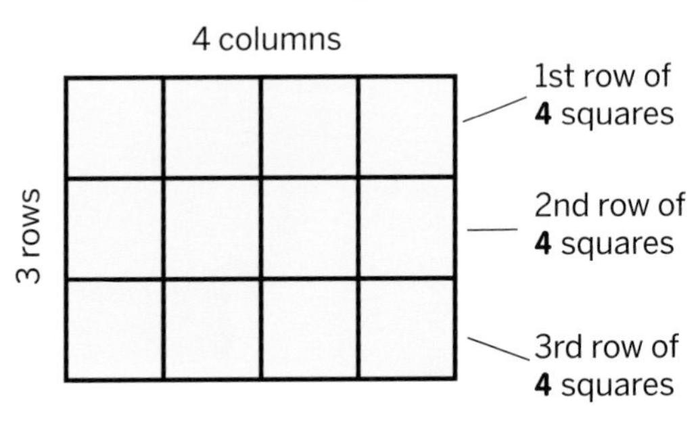

Mandy knew that multiplication was done by multiplying rows and columns. In this case there were **3** rows and **4** columns.

3 rows of 4 columns makes 12

As on the previous page, the calculation could be written as:

$$3 \times 4 = 12$$

Rearranging and multiplying

Having done this, Mandy rearranged the squares as shown below:

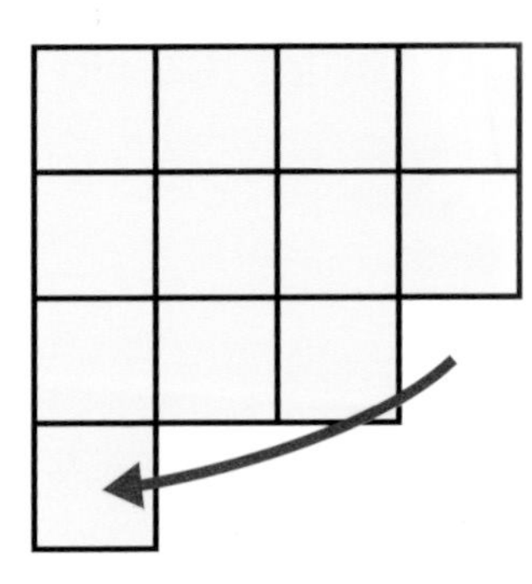

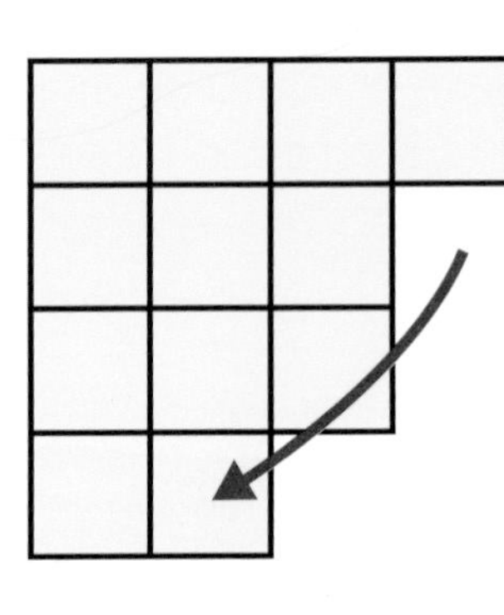

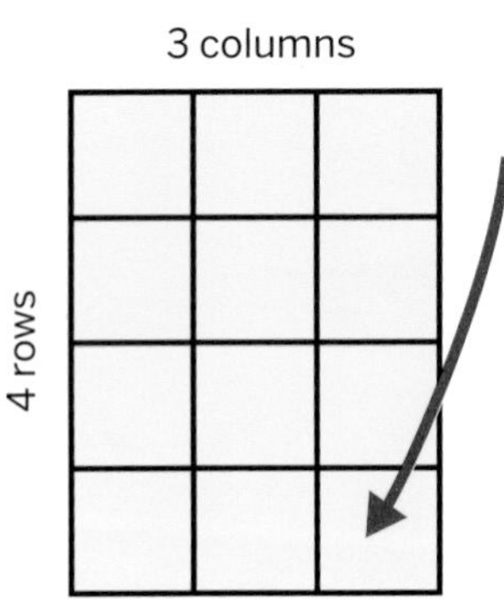

What she did was to move the blocks so that there were **4** rows and **3** columns. Mandy then said to herself:

4 rows of 3 columns makes 12

Which she knew could be written as:

$$4 \times 3 = 12$$

Jordan saved **£3** a week for **45** weeks. His Dad saved **£45** a week for **3** weeks to help pay for their holiday. Who had saved the most?

You would need a lot of squares to answer this as on the opposite page. You can probably see that you would get the same shape each time, just turned around (see below).

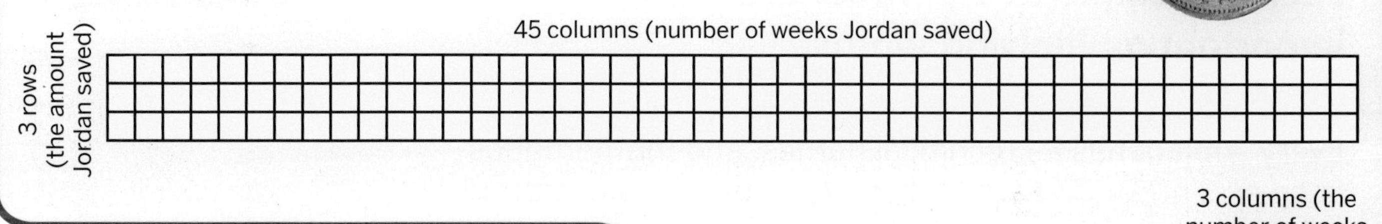

3 columns (the number of weeks Jordan's dad saved)

45 rows (the amount Jordan's dad saved)

Remember... Like adding, you can multiply in any order without affecting the result. This is called the Turn-Around Rule.

And, by the way, Mandy used a drawing to help her with the mathematics. The drawing made the mathematics easier to see.

That way we know that Jordan and his Dad had saved the same amount, even without knowing how much.

Use your calculator...

You can do all of these calculations on a calculator as well.

All multiplication operations use the '×' symbol on the calculator. You enter one of the numbers, say **3**, then press the multiplication sign (×) then enter the second number, say **4**, and finally press the equals sign (=). The answer is then displayed. You can see this shown below.

1. Enter **3**
2. Press multiplication sign (×)
3. Enter **4**
4. Press equals sign (=)

(Answer **12**)

Can you do this? Use a calculator, (see opposite) to find out how much they had saved, and to check the amounts are the same. (And see page 19 covering 'Short multiplication'.)

Factors, multiples and products

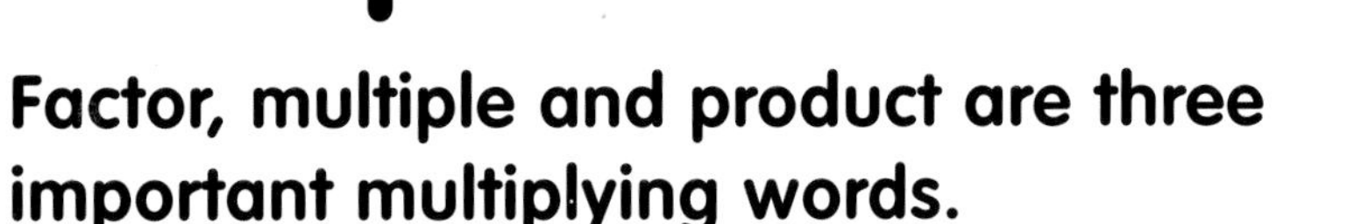

Factor, multiple and product are three important multiplying words.

Every subject has its technical names, and mathematics is no exception. So here we have to think our way around three multiplication words... factor, multiple and product.

Factor

This is the name for the numbers we multiply together. If we multiply **3 × 5**, then both **3** and **5** are called factors.

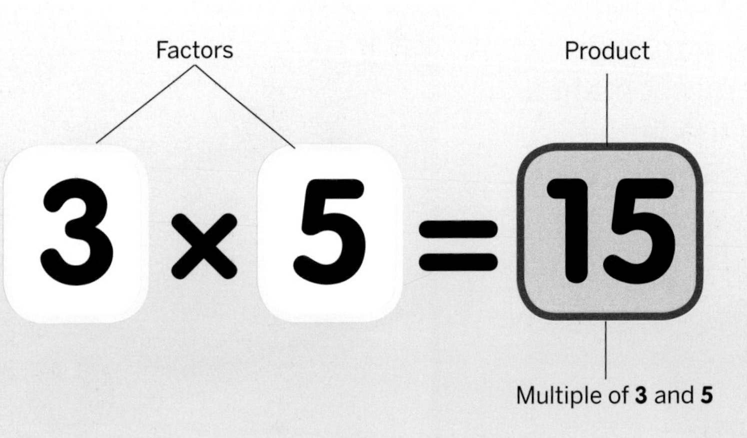

Multiple

All the numbers that can be obtained by multiplying by **3** are called multiples of **3**. The first ones are **2 × 3 = 6**; **3 × 3 = 9**; **4 × 3 = 12**; **5 × 3 = 15**; and so on for ever.

Describing a number like **117** as a multiple of **13** means that it comes from the list belonging to **13**. To say that **13** is a factor of **117** is another way of saying the same thing.

Product

When we multiply two numbers (factors) together we get an answer. When adding, we would use the word total. But when multiplying, the answer is called a product.

Remember... A product is made up of a pair of numbers multiplied together. A factor is the name for each of the numbers used in the multiplication.

Here are some more examples:

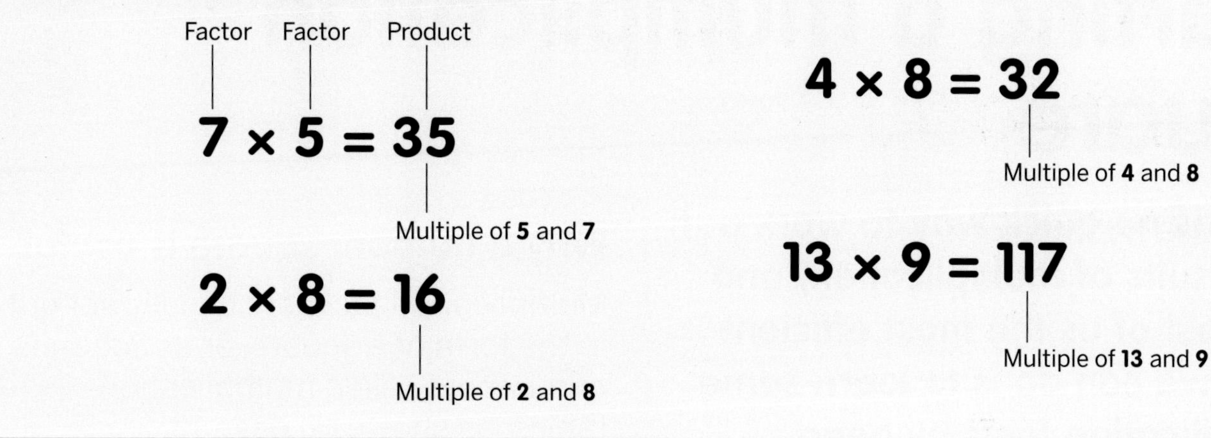

Fred's Dad bought an SUV for **£30,000**. As he did not have enough money, the sales person charged him interest at **£100** a year on every **£1,000** of the price for the whole agreement period, but with no deposit. He had to pay $1/4$ of the price each year for **4** years. How much had he paid at the end?

Do you think this was a good way of buying the car?

The price was **£30,000** which is **30 thousand pounds.**

So the interest each year was:

30 x £100 = £3,000

Dad had to pay this for four years.

4 x £3,000 = £12,000

By the end, the bill was:

SUV	**£30,000**
Deposit	**£0**
Interest	**£12,000**
TOTAL	**£42,000**

Fred's Dad should have considered a cheaper way of borrowing the money.

Use your calculator...

You can do all of these calculations on a calculator as well. For example, **13 × 9**, as shown below:

1. Enter **13**
2. Press multiplication sign (**×**)
3. Enter **9**
4. Press equals sign (**=**)

(Answer **117**)

Can you do this? On a separate piece of paper, make a list of all the factors of **24**.

Starting a multiplication square

There is no quick way to work out the results of multiplication, and for most of us the most efficient thing we can do is to learn some multiplication facts by heart.

Do you remember Jordan and his Dad who were saving for their holiday (page 9)?

Jordan started by saving some of his paper round money (page 4), and now he wanted to know if he had saved as much as his Dad.

Also, Lindsay had a vegetarian school lunch three times every week, and she wanted to know how many she had in a year (leaving out the school holidays).

Mathematically, that is actually the same problem as Jordan's.

To avoid a great deal of counting up we remember the most often used multiplication facts.

Finding them out once and writing the answer in our own table helps us to remember them, and gives us somewhere to look them up if we forget. You will probably need to look at your table many times.

Over the next few pages we are going to make our own table, and then find out how it helps us to multiply even bigger numbers to answer questions like Jordan's and Lindsay's.

Why a number square is useful

Multiplication facts are usually set out in the form of a square, or as columns of numbers called multiplication tables, as shown on page 16.

We are going to start to build a multiplication square using some of the numbers we obtained on the previous pages.

For example, on pages 6 and 7 we learned:

7 × 3 = 21 and **7 × 4 = 28**

On page 10 we also learned the Turn-Around Rule, so that

7 × 3 = 3 × 7 = 21

and

7 × 4 = 4 × 7 = 28

These four facts have been placed into a diagram that will build into a square-shaped table.

This table is made by writing the numbers **1** to **12** down the page and then across the page, as you can see below.

×	1	2	3	4	5	6	7	8	9	10	11	12
1												
2												
3												
4												
5												
6												
7												
8												
9												
10												
11												
12												

Finding your way about in the multiplication square:

1 Choose the first number from the top row and put your finger on it. In this case we have selected **3** and it has been marked with a blue circle.

2 Choose the second number from the left column and put another finger on it. In this case we have selected **7** and it has been marked with a green circle.

×	1	2	3	4	5	6	7	8	9	10	11	12
1												
2												
3							21					
4							28					
5												
6												
7			21	28								
8												
9												
10												
11												
12												

3 Run one finger down from the number top row, and the other across from the number in the left column until they meet. This is where we find the answer, **21**.

×	1	2	3	4	5	6	7	8	9	10	11	12
1												
2												
3							21					
4							28					
5												
6												
7			21	28								
8												
9												
10												
11												
12												

Remember... Knowing the Turn-Around Rule has already cut your learning almost in half. This is how we have been able to put four numbers on the square on this page when we have only worked out two results! The same is true for all other pairs of numbers.

Can you do this? Look back through the book to find answers we already know, and enter them into your copy of the table.

Completing the square

Much of the multiplication square can be completed by filling in more easy facts. Some examples of these are shown here. Filling in the square like this is useful because it shows you which numbers do not form parts of easy-to-learn patterns. These awkward numbers are shown in red on the page opposite.

Filling in 2's

The **2's** row and column was done by simply adding a number to itself. For example, **2 × 7** is the same as **7 + 7**. The answer is **14**.

×	1	2	3	4	5	6	7	8	9	10	11	12
1		2										
2	2	4	6	8	10	12	14	16	18	20	22	24
3		6					21					
4		8					28					
5		10										
6		12										
7		14	21	28								
8		16										
9		18										
10		20										
11		22										
12		24										

Filling in 1's, 6's, 10's, 11's and 12's

In this example the **1's**, **10's** and **11's** row and column have been completed. The **10's** row and column is just the **1's** row and column with a **0** on the end. The **11's** row and column is the **10's** and the **1's** added together.

A dozen means **12** and a half-dozen means **6**. Because we use these numbers a lot, we quickly remember answers.

×	1	2	3	4	5	6	7	8	9	10	11	12
1	1	2	3	4	5	6	7	8	9	10	11	12
2	2	4	6	8	10	12	14	16	18	20	22	24
3	3	6				18	21			30	33	36
4	4	8				24	28			40	44	48
5	5	10				30				50	55	60
6	6	12	18	24	30	36	42	48	54	60	66	72
7	7	14	21	28		42				70	77	84
8	8	16				48				80	88	96
9	9	18				54				90	99	108
10	10	20	30	40	50	60	70	80	90	100	110	120
11	11	22	33	44	55	66	77	88	99	110	121	132
12	12	24	36	48	60	72	84	96	108	120	132	144

Filling in 5's

Multiples of **5** all end in **5** or **0**.

Filling in results we already know such as:

4 × 3 = 12
3 × 4 = 12

×	1	2	3	4	5	6	7	8	9	10	11	12
1	1	2	3	4	5	6	7	8	9	10	11	12
2	2	4	6	8	10	12	14	16	18	20	22	24
3	3	6		12	15	18	21	24		30	33	36
4	4	8	12		20	24	28			40	44	48
5	5	10	15	20	25	30	35	40	45	50	55	60
6	6	12	18	24	30	36	42	48	54	60	66	72
7	7	14	21	28	35	42				70	77	84
8	8	16	24		40	48				80	88	96
9	9	18			45	54				90	99	108
10	10	20	30	40	50	60	70	80	90	100	110	120
11	11	22	33	44	55	66	77	88	99	110	121	132
12	12	24	36	48	60	72	84	96	108	120	132	144

The finished square

This finished square (right) has also had the square numbers added (see pages 24–25).

The numbers in red are the ones that many people find difficult to learn, so be sure to concentrate on remembering them!

×	1	2	3	4	5	6	7	8	9	10	11	12
1	1	2	3	4	5	6	7	8	9	10	11	12
2	2	4	6	8	10	12	14	16	18	20	22	24
3	3	6	9	12	15	18	21	24	27	30	33	36
4	4	8	12	16	20	24	28	32	36	40	44	48
5	5	10	15	20	25	30	35	40	45	50	55	60
6	6	12	18	24	30	36	42	48	54	60	66	72
7	7	14	21	28	35	42	49	56	63	70	77	84
8	8	16	24	32	40	48	56	64	72	80	88	96
9	9	18	27	36	45	54	63	72	81	90	99	108
10	10	20	30	40	50	60	70	80	90	100	110	120
11	11	22	33	44	55	66	77	88	99	110	121	132
12	12	24	36	48	60	72	84	96	108	120	132	144

Remember... The multiplication square is made up of simple multiplication facts, as you can see.

▼ The complete multiplication square.

×	1	2	3	4	5	6	7	8	9	10	11	12
1	1	2	3	4	5	6	7	8	9	10	11	12
2	2	4	6	8	10	12	14	16	18	20	22	24
3	3	6	9	12	15	18	21	24	27	30	33	36
4	4	8	12	16	20	24	28	32	36	40	44	48
5	5	10	15	20	25	30	35	40	45	50	55	60
6	6	12	18	24	30	36	42	48	54	60	66	72
7	7	14	21	28	35	42	49	56	63	70	77	84
8	8	16	24	32	40	48	56	64	72	80	88	96
9	9	18	27	36	45	54	63	72	81	90	99	108
10	10	20	30	40	50	60	70	80	90	100	110	120
11	11	22	33	44	55	66	77	88	99	110	121	132
12	12	24	36	48	60	72	84	96	108	120	132	144

Can you do this? Turn the tables on your friends! Who can get ten out of ten tables questions right in 30 seconds?

Multiplication tables

Your 'times tables' come from a multiplication square.

Multiplication facts can be set out as a square or as columns of numbers called multiplication tables, or 'times tables'. It is easier to see patterns in multiplication squares, but multiplication tables are easier to learn by heart.

▶ **12 × 12** square

×	1	2	3	4	5	6	7	8	9	10	11	12
1	1	2	3	4	5	6	7	8	9	10	11	12
2	2	4	6	8	10	12	14	16	18	20	22	24
3	3	6	9	12	15	18	21	24	27	30	33	36
4	4	8	12	16	20	24	28	32	36	40	44	48
5	5	10	15	20	25	30	35	40	45	50	55	60
6	6	12	18	24	30	36	42	48	54	60	66	72
7	7	14	21	28	35	42	49	56	63	70	77	84
8	8	16	24	32	40	48	56	64	72	80	88	96
9	9	18	27	36	45	54	63	72	81	90	99	108
10	10	20	30	40	50	60	70	80	90	100	110	120
11	11	22	33	44	55	66	77	88	99	110	121	132
12	12	24	36	48	60	72	84	96	108	120	132	144

This is the column used to make the **7** times table.

1	x	7	=	7
2	x	7	=	14
3	x	7	=	21
4	x	7	=	28
5	x	7	=	35
6	x	7	=	42
7	x	7	=	49
8	x	7	=	56
9	x	7	=	63
10	x	7	=	70
11	x	7	=	77
12	x	7	=	84

▶ This shows you how the **7** times table is related to a multiplication square.

Remember... The Turn-Around Rule (**8 x 2** is the same as **2 x 8** etc) helps you to understand that you only have to learn about half as many numbers as are in multiplication tables.

2	3	4	5	6	7
1 × 2 = 2	1 × 3 = 3	1 × 4 = 4	1 × 5 = 5	1 × 6 = 6	1 × 7 = 7
2 × 2 = 4	2 × 3 = 6	2 × 4 = 8	2 × 5 = 10	2 × 6 = 12	2 × 7 = 14
3 × 2 = 6	3 × 3 = 9	3 × 4 = 12	3 × 5 = 15	3 × 6 = 18	3 × 7 = 21
4 × 2 = 8	4 × 3 = 12	4 × 4 = 16	4 × 5 = 20	4 × 6 = 24	4 × 7 = 28
5 × 2 = 10	5 × 3 = 15	5 × 4 = 20	5 × 5 = 25	5 × 6 = 30	5 × 7 = 35
6 × 2 = 12	6 × 3 = 18	6 × 4 = 24	6 × 5 = 30	6 × 6 = 36	6 × 7 = 42
7 × 2 = 14	7 × 3 = 21	7 × 4 = 28	7 × 5 = 35	7 × 6 = 42	7 × 7 = 49
8 × 2 = 16	8 × 3 = 24	8 × 4 = 32	8 × 5 = 40	8 × 6 = 48	8 × 7 = 56
9 × 2 = 18	9 × 3 = 27	9 × 4 = 36	9 × 5 = 45	9 × 6 = 54	9 × 7 = 63
10 × 2 = 20	10 × 3 = 30	10 × 4 = 40	10 × 5 = 50	10 × 6 = 60	10 × 7 = 70
11 × 2 = 22	11 × 3 = 33	11 × 4 = 44	11 × 5 = 55	11 × 6 = 66	11 × 7 = 77
12 × 2 = 24	12 × 3 = 36	12 × 4 = 48	12 × 5 = 60	12 × 6 = 72	12 × 7 = 84

8	9	10	11	12
1 × 8 = 8	1 × 9 = 9	1 × 10 = 10	1 × 11 = 11	1 × 12 = 12
2 × 8 = 16	2 × 9 = 18	2 × 10 = 20	2 × 11 = 22	2 × 12 = 24
3 × 8 = 24	3 × 9 = 27	3 × 10 = 30	3 × 11 = 33	3 × 12 = 36
4 × 8 = 32	4 × 9 = 36	4 × 10 = 40	4 × 11 = 44	4 × 12 = 48
5 × 8 = 40	5 × 9 = 45	5 × 10 = 50	5 × 11 = 55	5 × 12 = 60
6 × 8 = 48	6 × 9 = 54	6 × 10 = 60	6 × 11 = 66	6 × 12 = 72
7 × 8 = 56	7 × 9 = 63	7 × 10 = 70	7 × 11 = 77	7 × 12 = 84
8 × 8 = 64	8 × 9 = 72	8 × 10 = 80	8 × 11 = 88	8 × 12 = 96
9 × 8 = 72	9 × 9 = 81	9 × 10 = 90	9 × 11 = 99	9 × 12 = 108
10 × 8 = 80	10 × 9 = 90	10 × 10 = 100	10 × 11 = 110	10 × 12 = 120
11 × 8 = 88	11 × 9 = 99	11 × 10 = 110	11 × 11 = 121	11 × 12 = 132
12 × 8 = 96	12 × 9 = 108	12 × 10 = 120	12 × 11 = 132	12 × 12 = 144

Can you do this? Your aim should be to give the correct answer to any multiplication fact up to **12 × 12** without having to think.

Short multiplication

Use short multiplication when one number is 9 or less.

First organise the numbers into columns. We have used colours to help you to keep track of the values of each column.
To do short multiplication, multiply each number on the top, by the number on the bottom, starting at the right.

The party

Sarah was going to give out invitations for a party to be held in the local hall. The hall had **14** tables that would each seat **8** guests. So Sarah had to find out the number of guests she could invite. For this she used short multiplication.

1

Write one number above the other, and line them both up to the right in columns.

Draw a line below them. The product, or answer, of the multiplication is then written below the line.

In this example we are multiplying **14 × 8**, and so we write **8** below the **4** in **14**. This is because both the **4** and the **8** are units (remember that **14** is actually **1** ten and **4** units).

▼ The problem written as a row.

14 × 8 = ?

▶ The same problem rearranged and placed onto coloured columns.

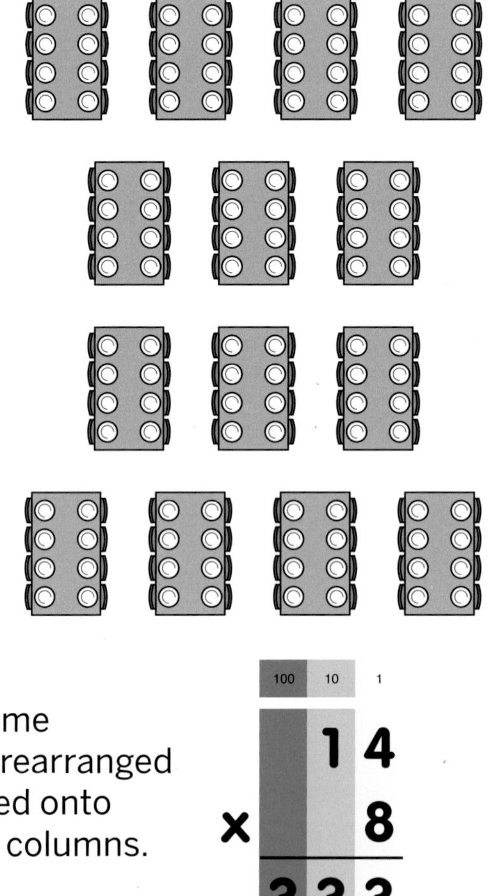

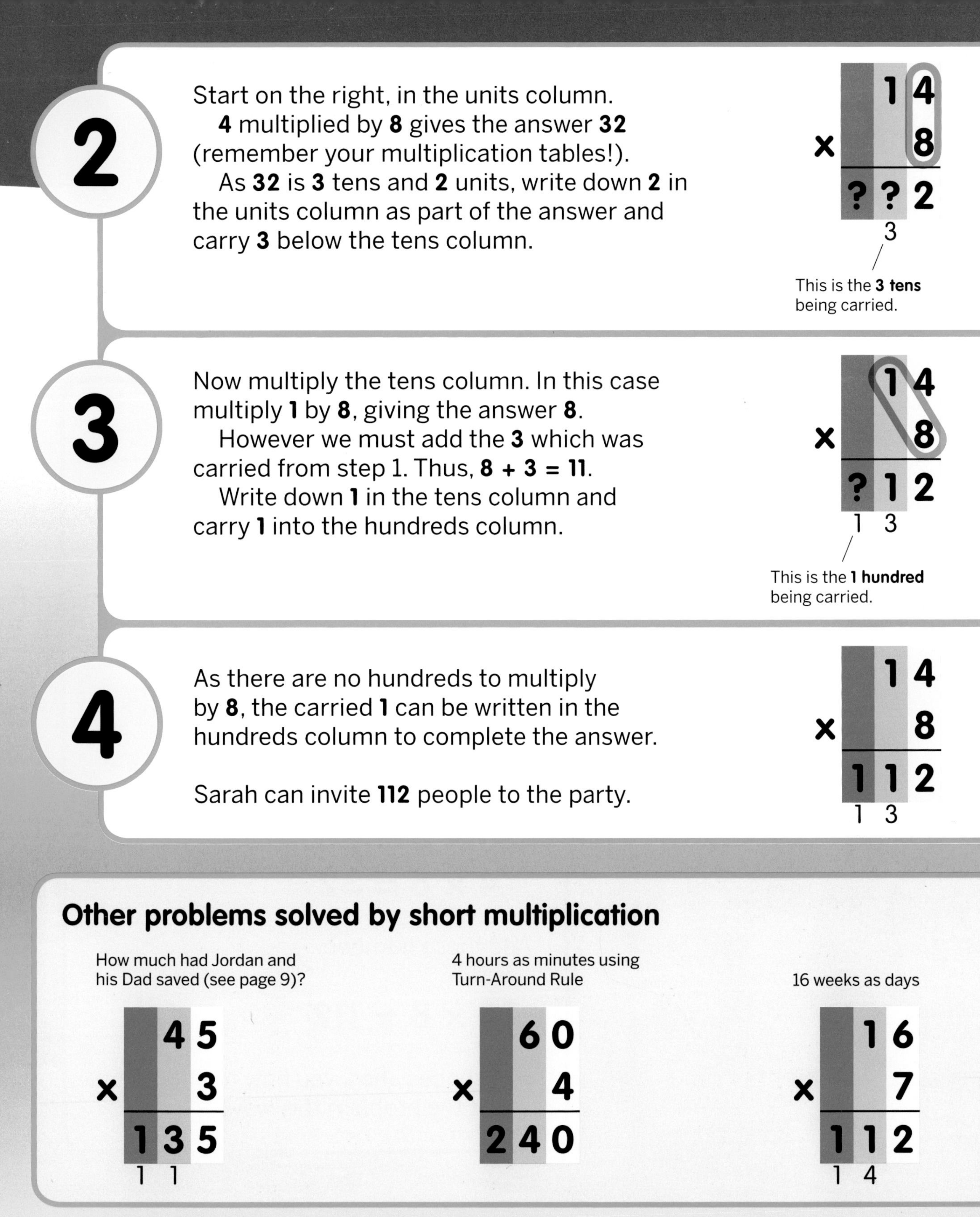

2

Start on the right, in the units column.
4 multiplied by **8** gives the answer **32** (remember your multiplication tables!).
As **32** is **3** tens and **2** units, write down **2** in the units column as part of the answer and carry **3** below the tens column.

3

Now multiply the tens column. In this case multiply **1** by **8**, giving the answer **8**.
However we must add the **3** which was carried from step 1. Thus, **8 + 3 = 11**.
Write down **1** in the tens column and carry **1** into the hundreds column.

4

As there are no hundreds to multiply by **8**, the carried **1** can be written in the hundreds column to complete the answer.

Sarah can invite **112** people to the party.

Other problems solved by short multiplication

Can you do this? Try to do short multiplications like the ones on this page faster than someone using a calculator.

Remember... Follow the rules. Put one number above the other, lining them up to the right using columns. In short multiplication, multiply the larger number by the number with a single digit.

More short multiplication

You can use grids and shapes to help multiply.

There is usually a variety of ways to solve a problem. This is what Narindar discovered when he wanted to find out the number of guests he could fit into a friend's restaurant. The problem is the same one that Sarah had on page 18, but the answer is laid out in two different patterns. Work with the one that suits you best.

Example 1:
Split up the problem

14 is made up of one **10** and **4** units.

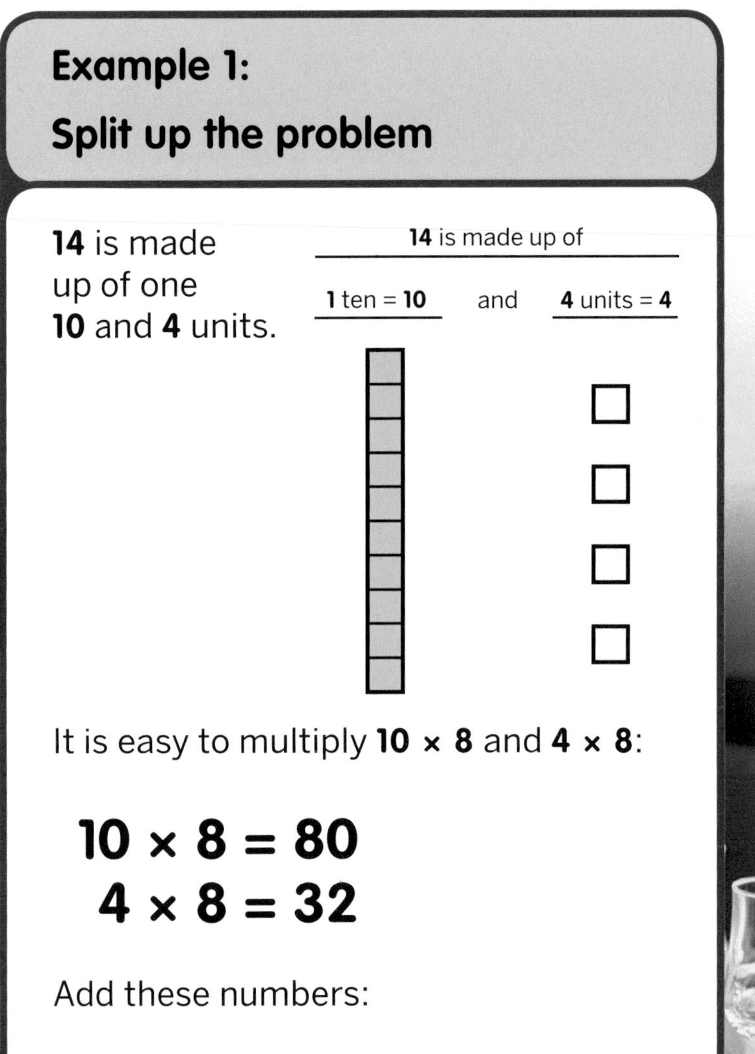

It is easy to multiply **10 × 8** and **4 × 8**:

10 × 8 = 80
4 × 8 = 32

Add these numbers:

14 × 8 = 112

The shapes show you how to think about the problem this way.

Example 2:

Using grids

There is another way:

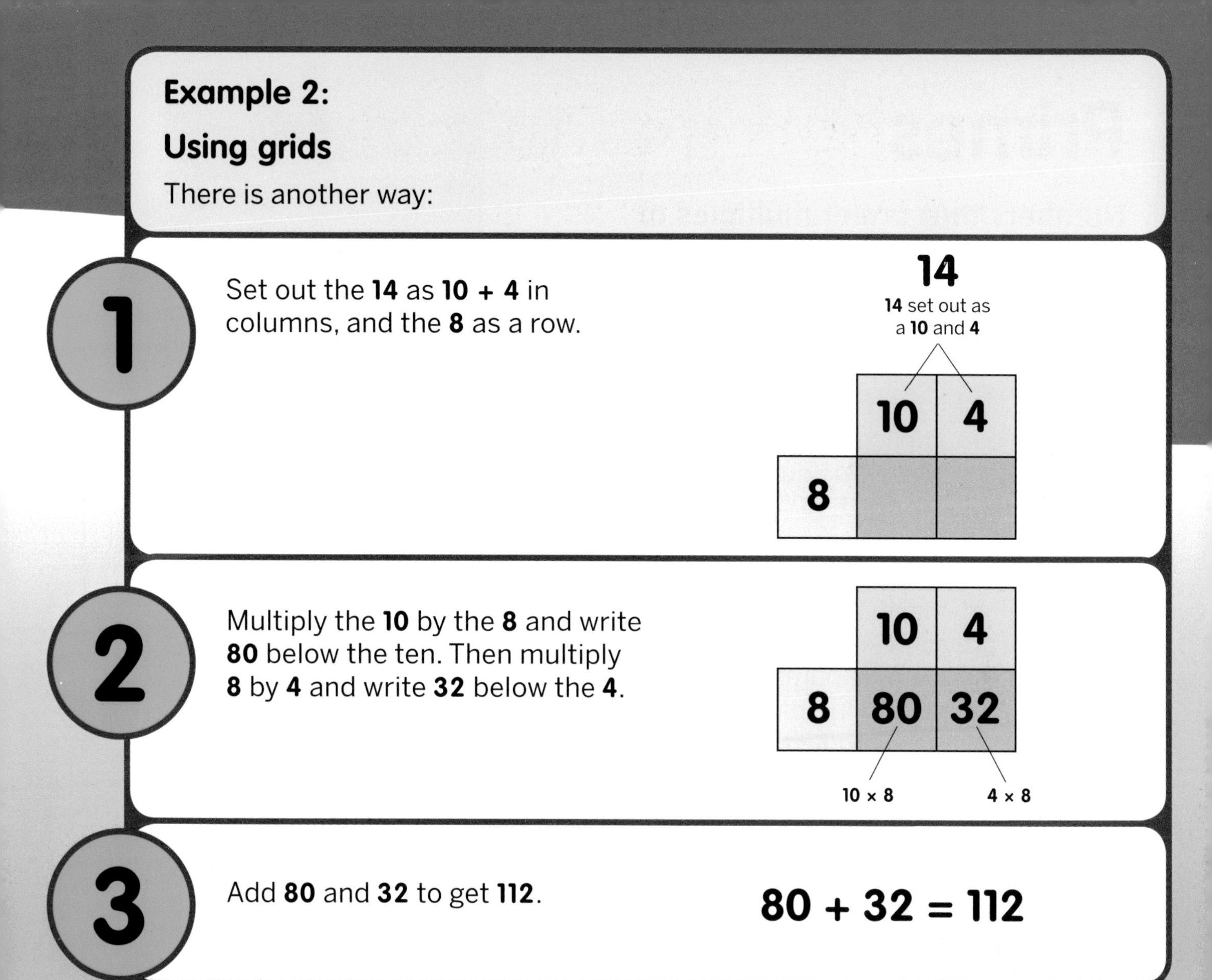

1 Set out the **14** as **10 + 4** in columns, and the **8** as a row.

2 Multiply the **10** by the **8** and write **80** below the ten. Then multiply **8** by **4** and write **32** below the **4**.

3 Add **80** and **32** to get **112**.

80 + 32 = 112

Remember... The Turn-Around Rule means you can multiply in any order without affecting the result.

Can you do this? There are **365** days in a year, except every fourth year (a leap year) has an extra day. How many days old were you on your fourth birthday?

Work the answer out on a separate piece of paper.

Primes

Numbers that aren't multiples of smaller numbers are primes.

Some numbers are not multiples of smaller numbers. They are called prime numbers. When prime numbers are used as part of a multiplication, they are called prime factors. The prime numbers less than **20** are **2**, **3**, **5**, **7**, **11**, **13**, **17** and **19**.

When multiplying, it is important to know that there are some special numbers, called prime numbers. Prime numbers are the building numbers of multiplication. They cannot be split into products of two smaller numbers without using **1**. For example, although the number **4** can be made by multiplying **2 × 2**, the number **5** cannot be made by multiplying together any smaller whole numbers without using **1**, and so it is a prime number. If we used **1**, we could use it every time, and there would be no prime numbers left. That is why we do not use **1**.

Both **3** and **5** are prime factors of **15** because both **3** and **5** are multiplied together to make **15**, but neither **3** or **5** can themselves be made from smaller whole numbers.

In a similar way the numbers **3** and **7** are prime factors of **21**. Clearly, the product of a multiplication can never be a prime number because it is calculated from two factors.

Examples

Prime factors (a factor that cannot be made by multiplying together any smaller numbers).

Product (a number that is made by multiplying two smaller numbers).

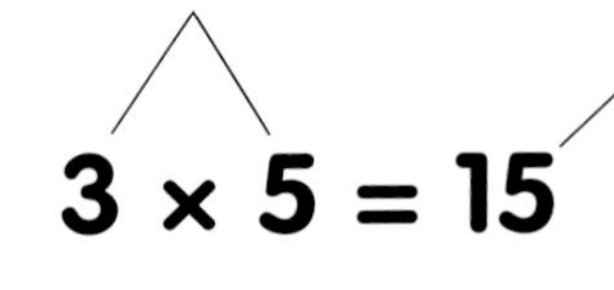

Prime factor

3 × 4 = 12

Multiple of **2**, so not a prime number.

Prime factors

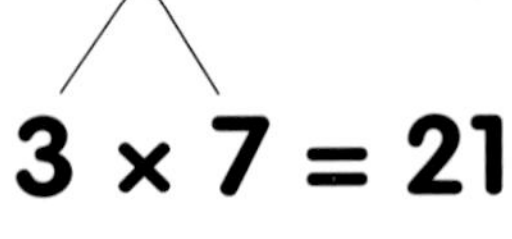

Can you do this? **7**, **11** and **13** are all prime numbers. Use a calculator to multiply them together. Try some other primes.

Finding prime numbers

You can find prime numbers up to any size simply by using a table made of all the numbers in order. This is called the Sieve of Eratosthenes, after its inventor. A table of numbers up to **100** is shown here with the prime numbers on the red squares.

1	2	3	4	5	6	7	8	9	10
11	12	13	14	15	16	17	18	19	20
21	22	23	24	25	26	27	28	29	30
31	32	33	34	35	36	37	38	39	40
41	42	43	44	45	46	47	48	49	50
51	52	53	54	55	56	57	58	59	60
61	62	63	64	65	66	67	68	69	70
71	72	73	74	75	76	77	78	79	80
81	82	83	84	85	86	87	88	89	90
91	92	93	94	95	96	97	98	99	100

Copy this table to see how it works. Start by circling **2**, which is the smallest prime number (we don't use **1**). Any multiple of **2** cannot be a prime number. So go on in jumps of **2** crossing out **4**, **6**, **8**, **10** etc. to **100**.

Now circle **3**, the next smallest prime number. Any multiple of **3** cannot be a prime number. Move on in jumps of **3**, crossing out **9**, **15**, **21**, **27** etc.

And so we go on. Circle **5**, then go in jumps of **5**, crossing any uncrossed multiple (**25**, **35** etc.).

Circle **7**, go in jumps of **7**, crossing any uncrossed multiple (only **49** and **77** left).

And that completes the sieve. Every number left is a prime number.

Goldbach's Conjecture

The number **2** is the only prime number that is even. Can you explain why?

In 1742, Christian Goldbach stated that all other even numbers can be obtained by adding together exactly two primes. To this day, nobody has found an even number for which this cannot be done. But nobody has ever been able to explain why Goldbach's Conjecture is always correct either.

Remember... Prime numbers are those that are not multiples of others (**2**, **3**, **5**, **7** etc.). Prime factors are the prime numbers used in multiplication (for example, **2 × 2 × 5 = 20**; the prime factors are **2** and **5**.

Can you do this? Check out Goldbach's Conjecture for **4**, **6**, **8** … and several more small even numbers.

Square numbers and square roots

When a whole number is multiplied by itself, for example, 4 × 4, the result is called a square number.

There are some whole numbers that are special. These are called square numbers.

Every square number can be produced by multiplying a number by itself. For example, if we multiply **2 ×** **2** we get **4**. In this example, **4** is the square number.

The number used to make a square number in this way is called a square root. In the case of **2 × 2 = 4**, the square root number of **4** is **2**.

Similarly, multiplying **3** by itself makes **9**. So **9** is the square number, and **3** is its square root.

Multiplying **4** by itself makes **16**. So **16** is the square number, and **4** is its square root. Multiplying **5** by itself makes **25**. So **25** is the square number and **5** is its square root.

You can see these examples set out in shapes on the right.

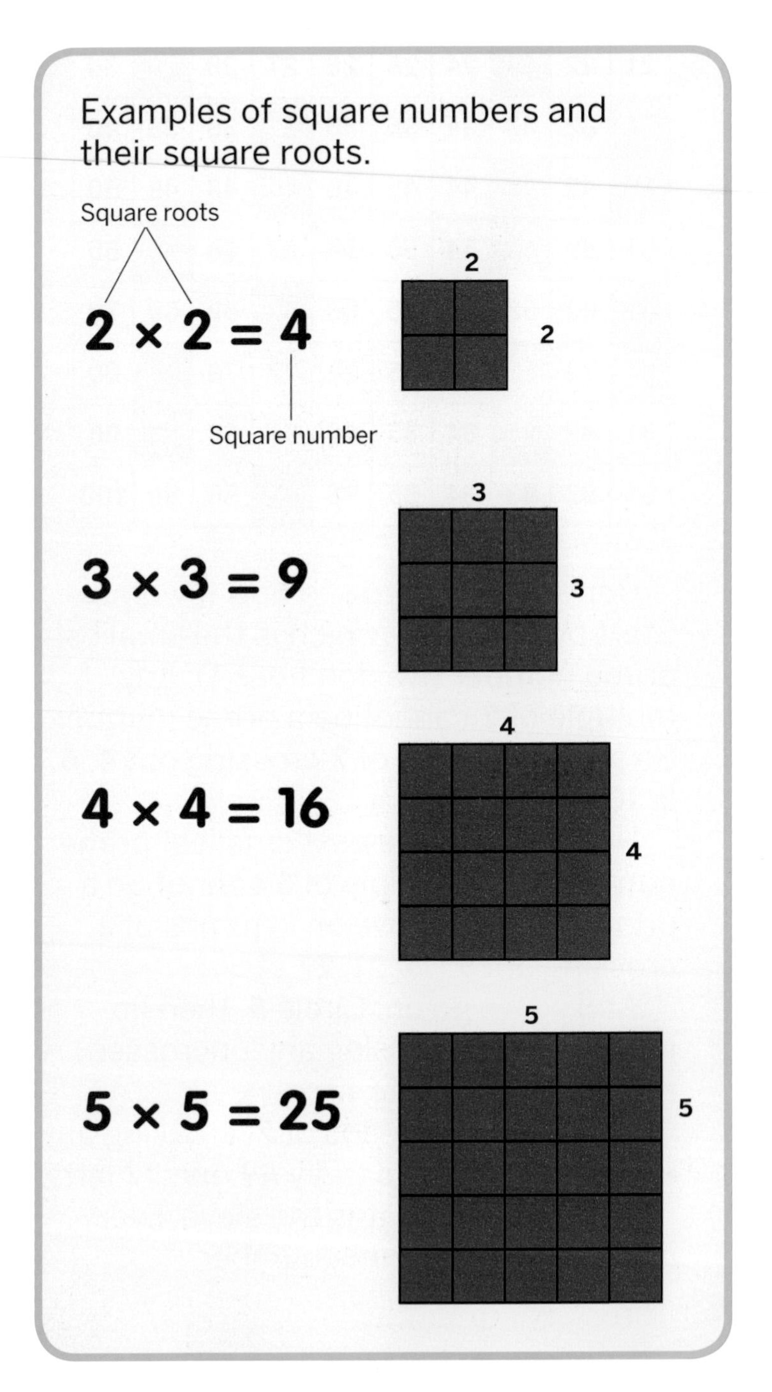

Other factors in square numbers

Square numbers can often be obtained without using the square roots. For example, **6 × 6 = 36**, but **36** is also **9 × 4**. But each square number only has one square root, and it is always a whole number.

Square roots of other numbers

Every number has a square root, although only square numbers have square roots that are whole numbers. For example, **15** is a whole number, but it is not a square number because it is not the product of a number multiplied by itself.

The square root of **15** is therefore not a whole number. Using a calculator, you would find that the square root of **15** is:

3.8729833

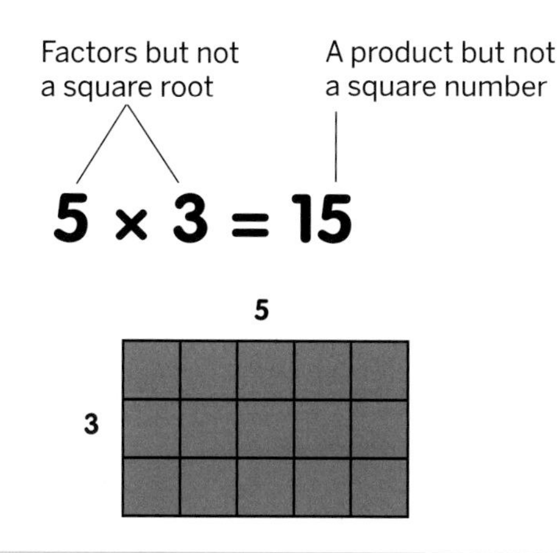

Finding a square root using your calculator...
Many calculators have buttons that will calculate square roots automatically. Every positive number has a square root, but only some have square roots that are whole numbers.

You can use your calculator to experiment to find out which numbers have exact square roots. For example, if you enter the number **36** and press the square root sign, the answer is **6** exactly. So **6** is an exact square root of **36** and **36** is a square number:

1. Enter **36**
2. Press square root sign (√)

(Answer reads **6**)

Remember... The square root of a square number is always a whole number.

Mathematicians use special signs for squares and square roots.

$$3 \times 3 = 9$$

can be written as

$3^2 = 9$ which is said "**three squared equals nine.**"

In reverse, "**the square root of nine equals three**" can be written

$$\sqrt{9} = 3$$

√ is called the square root sign.

Can you do this?

On a piece of paper write down the missing square number, and also the square roots of these spooky numbers.

(Look at page 24 and page 15.)

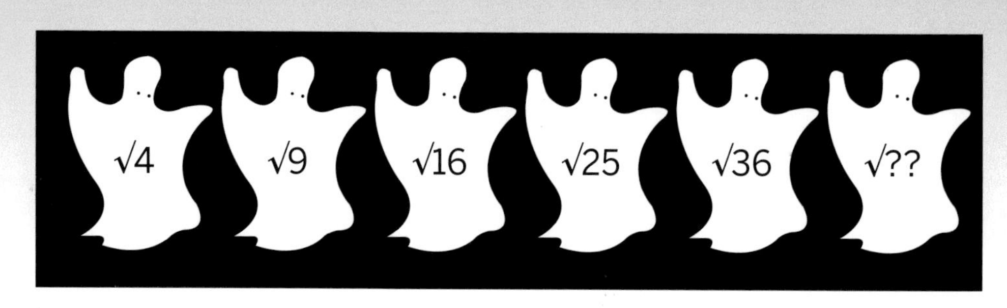

Multiplying and adding

Sometimes problems involve both multiplying and adding. In this case we do have to do them in the right order. Here you see how Ziggie was clever in tackling this kind of problem.

Ziggie and the crown jewels

Ziggie, her mother and father, and her five brothers and sisters, went to visit the Tower of London. They arrived at the gate and found that the cost of entry was **£9**. But they also wanted to see the crown jewels, which were in the Bloody Tower, where many years ago lots of famous people were locked up before being executed. For this they had to pay an extra **£4**. While they waited in the queue, Ziggie tried to help her father to work out what he would have to pay when he got to the cashier.

Setting out the problem

Ziggie's father had to pay **£9** and **£4** for each of the eight people in his family. How much did he have to pay altogether? To find the answer he had to add two separate multiplications:

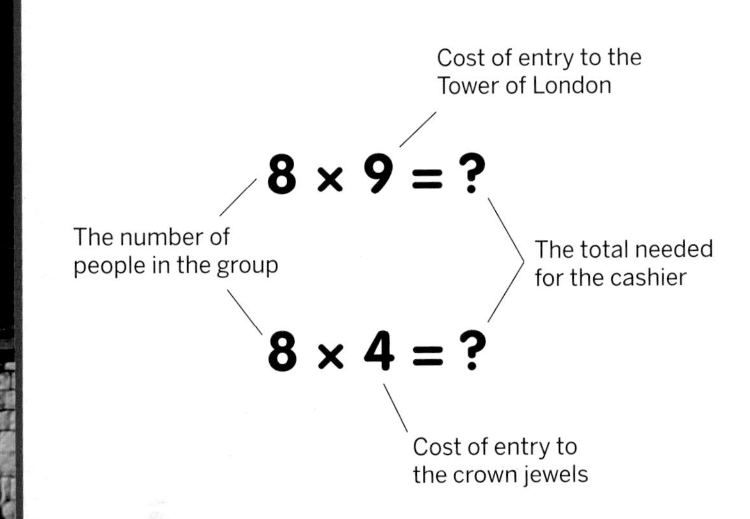

Multiplying then adding

Using her multiplication tables (which Ziggie had learned by heart at school, but which are also on page 17):

$$8 \times 9 = 72$$

and

$$8 \times 4 = 32$$

so

$$72 + 32 = 104$$

Adding then multiplying

Ziggie thought it would be easier to work it out like this:

Each person had to pay **£9** and **£4**, so:

$$9 + 4 = 13$$

and

$$8 \times 13 = 104$$

Calculating in her head

As Ziggie was standing in a queue, she wanted to be able to work out the answer in her head. So, as **9 + 4** is the same as **10 + 3** she could split her working out into:

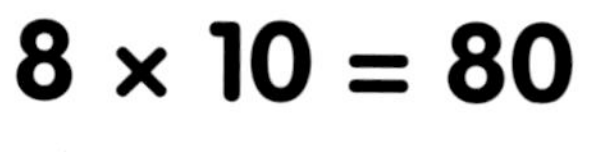

$$8 \times 10 = 80$$

and

$$8 \times 3 = 24$$

so

$$80 + 24 = 104$$

Ziggie's father had to pay **£104**.

Can you do this?
The next day Ziggie and her family went on a London river cruise. Adult tickets cost **£10.50**, children's were half price. Ziggie found an easy way to work out how much her Dad had to pay for two adults and six children. Can you?

Long multiplication by columns

Multiplying together numbers bigger than 9 needs long multiplication. Here we use columns.

1

Place one number above the other, lining up the numbers to the right so that units line up with units, tens line up with tens and so on. Draw a line below the numbers. The working will go below this line.

100	10	1
	3	8
×	1	4
?	?	?

2

Multiply each part of the top number by each of the digits of the lower number in turn.

Multiply from the right. **4 × 8 = 32**, so we write **2** in the units column and carry a small **3** below the tens column, to add to the tens when we have worked them out.

	3	8
×	1	4
?	?	2
	3	

This is the **3 tens** carried over.

3

Now multiply the **3** by the **4** (**3 × 4 = 12**). Adding the carried over **3** makes a total of **15**. Write **5** in the tens column and carry forward a small **1** into the hundreds column.

In fact, there are no other hundreds, so this **1** can be written next to the **5**, making **152**.

	3	8
×	1	4
1	5	2
1	3	

This is the **1 hundred** carried over.

Remember... Line up the numbers to the right, one below the other. Start with the units and do a short multiplication. Move on to the tens, put a zero on the right of the line below and do another short multiplication. Then add the results.

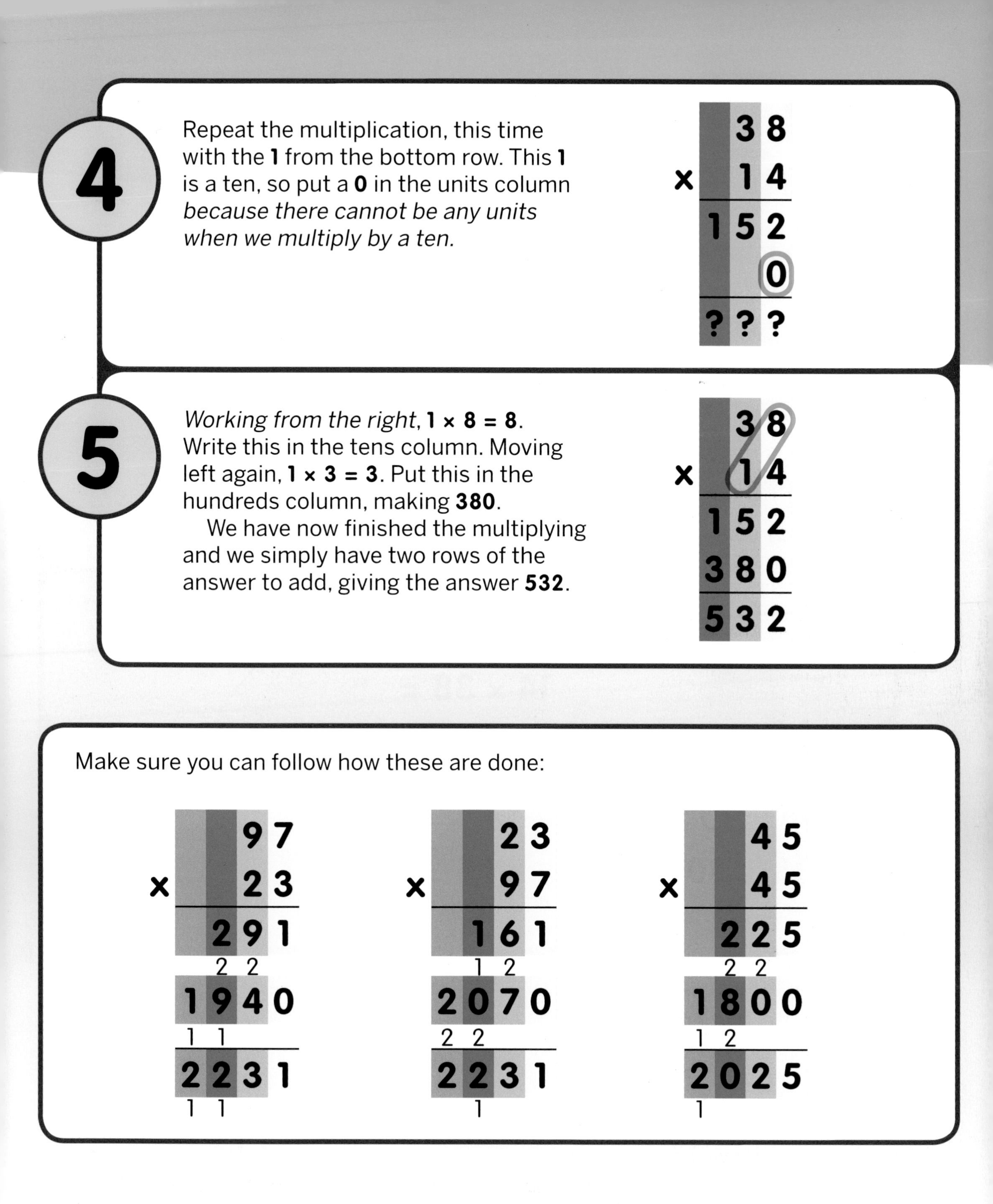

Can you do this? If we started from the left, multiplying by the tens first, then by the units, would it work just as well?

Explain your answer on a separate piece of paper.

Long multiplying by grids

Multiplying together numbers bigger than 9 needs long multiplication. Here we use grids.

Problem

Wendy is working part time in a supermarket and has been stacking a display shelf. The manager asked her how many items she had used so that he could keep a proper record of stock.

Wendy could have counted the items, but as the items were stacked up in rows, she knew that it would be much faster to count the rows and columns of the display and then multiply these two numbers together.

She quickly counted up the number of rows as **14** and the number of columns as **38**. But then she had to multiply them together:

14 × 38 =

1

Separate out the numbers so they are easier to work with.

14 is 10 + 4

38 is 30 + 8

2

Place the separated numbers in the border of a grid (blue squares) as we did for short multiplication on page 21. Notice that in this case there are **2** rows because the number we are multiplying with has **2** digits.

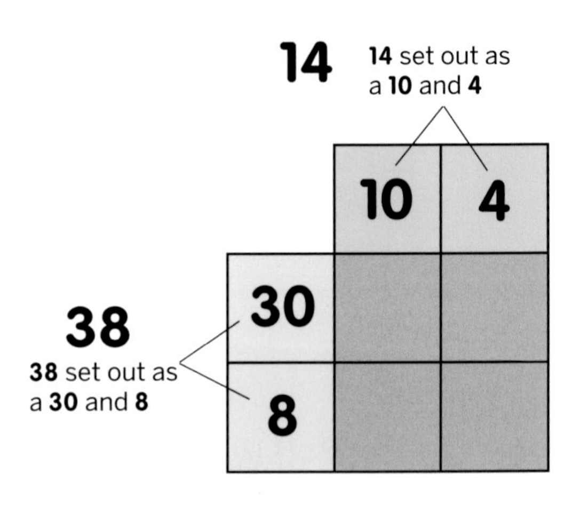

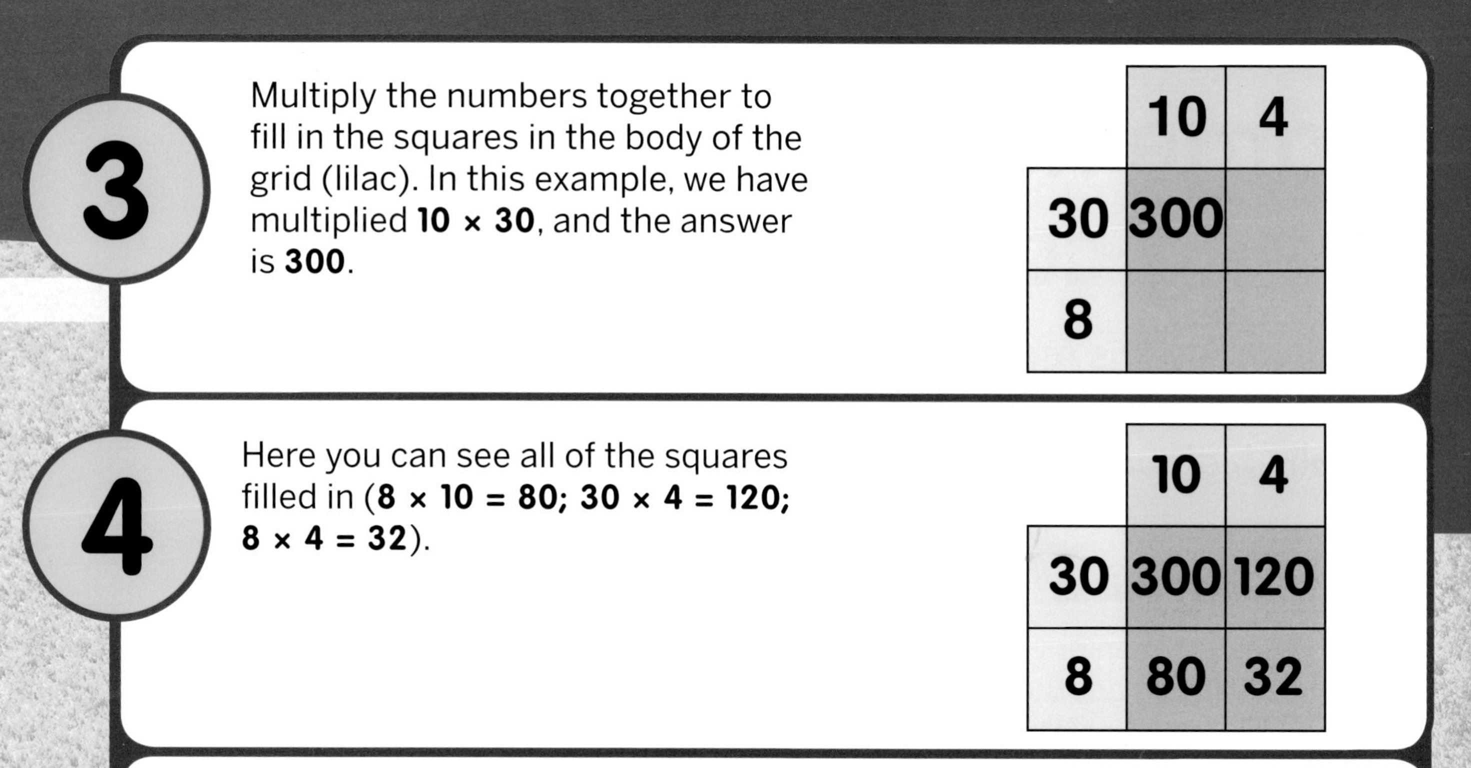

3

Multiply the numbers together to fill in the squares in the body of the grid (lilac). In this example, we have multiplied **10 × 30**, and the answer is **300**.

	10	4
30	300	
8		

4

Here you can see all of the squares filled in (**8 × 10 = 80; 30 × 4 = 120; 8 × 4 = 32**).

	10	4
30	300	120
8	80	32

5

Last of all, add all the numbers in the (lilac) 'body' squares:

300 + 120 + 80 + 32 = 532

So Wendy had stacked **532** items in the display.

What is the biggest allowed area of a soccer pitch?

It can measure up to **119 m x 91 m**. Its area is found (in square metres) by multiplying the length by the width.

Using the grid method (see opposite).

	100	10	9
90	9,000	900	810
1	100	10	9

Now we add the 'body' numbers of the grid.

9,000 + 900 + 810 + 100 + 10 + 9 = 10,829

The biggest allowed area of a soccer pitch is **10,829 m²**.

(To give you an idea of size, **10,000 m² = 1 hectare**.)

Remember... You can use grids to multiply big numbers together, but first separate the numbers into tens, units etc. When the grid is filled in, just add the numbers in the 'body' squares of the grid to find the total.

Can you do this? What is the smallest allowed area of a soccer pitch? It must be at least **91 m x 46 m**.

Work the answer out on a separate piece of paper.

Large numbers using columns

You can use as many hidden columns as you need to multiply really big numbers.

How many bricks?

Gavin had a wall along one side of his garden and he wanted to build another one to match it. But to do this he had to order the bricks first. Gavin needed to know how many bricks to order.

In his existing wall there were **27** levels (builders call these levels 'courses'). There were **109** bricks in the top course (and all courses have the same number of bricks).

To find the number of bricks to order multiply the number of bricks in the length (**109**) by the number in the height (**27**).

109 × 27 = ?

Here is the multiplication set out as a long multiplication using the method on page 28. However, in this case we will multiply by the tens first and the units last – just to show you it makes no difference.

	1000	100	10	1
		1	0	9
×			2	7
	?	?	?	?

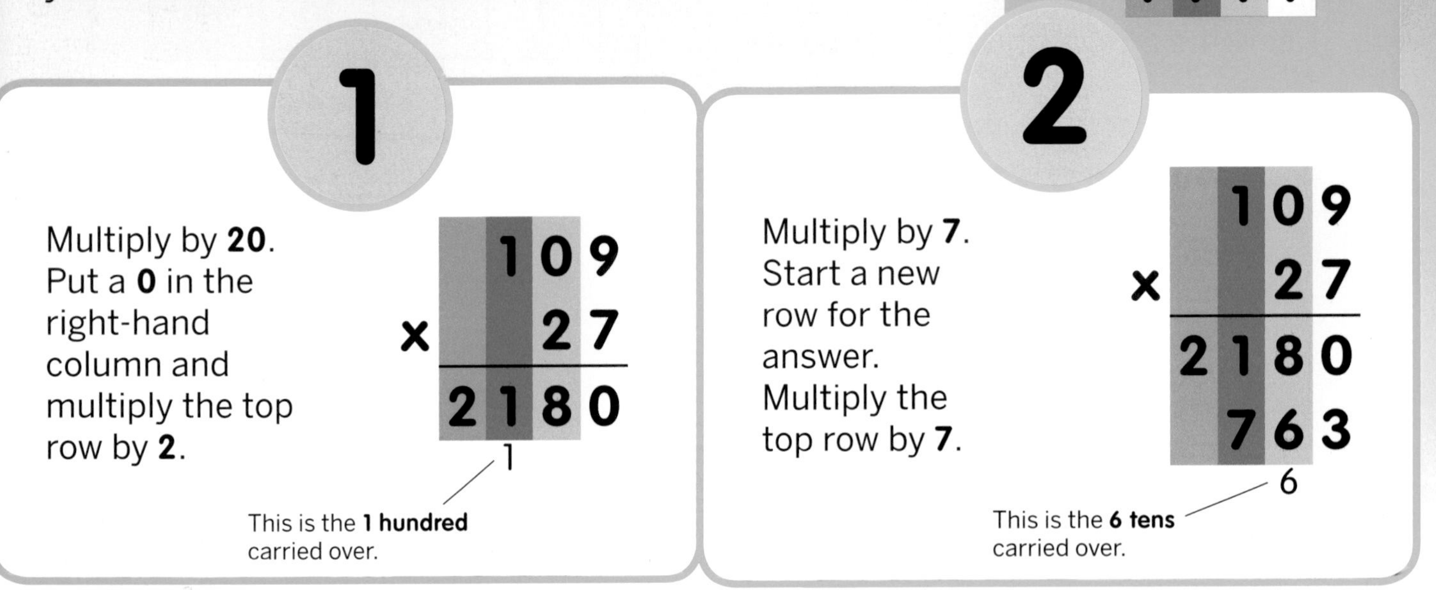

3

Add the results.

```
   109
 x  27
 -----
  2180
   763
 -----
  2943
   1
```

This is the **1 hundred** carried over.

Answer: Gavin needs to order **2,943** bricks.

William's parents have not been managing their money well. They are in debt to the bank, and the bank manager wants them to pay back **£275** a month for **24** months. How much must they repay?

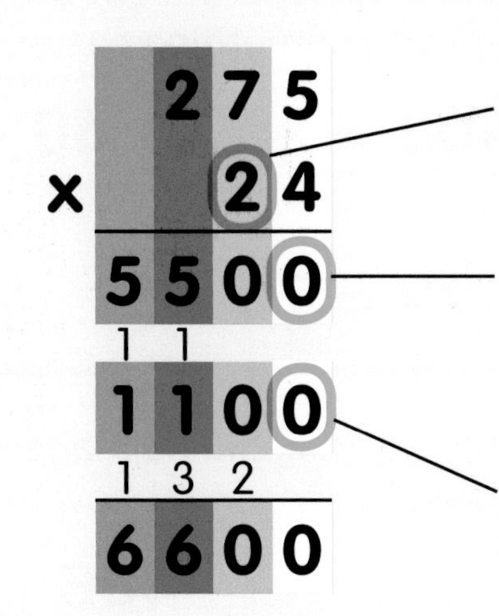

Again we start with the **2** of **24** (to show it makes no difference).

The right hand **0** is because we are really multiplying by **20**, not by **2** (we call it a 'place holder'), but the next **0** comes from **2 x 5 = 10**.

Here the right hand **0** comes from **4 x 5 = 20**.

They must repay **£6,600**.

Remember... To choose a method that suits you. Here you can see that you can multiply long numbers directly, line by line, or you can split the numbers up and make it easier to multiply. Choose whichever method suits you – they all give the same answer, of course!

Can you do these?

286 x 116 = ?

156 x 437 = ?

Work the answers out on a separate piece of paper.

Large numbers using grids

Three-digit numbers can be multiplied using a grid.

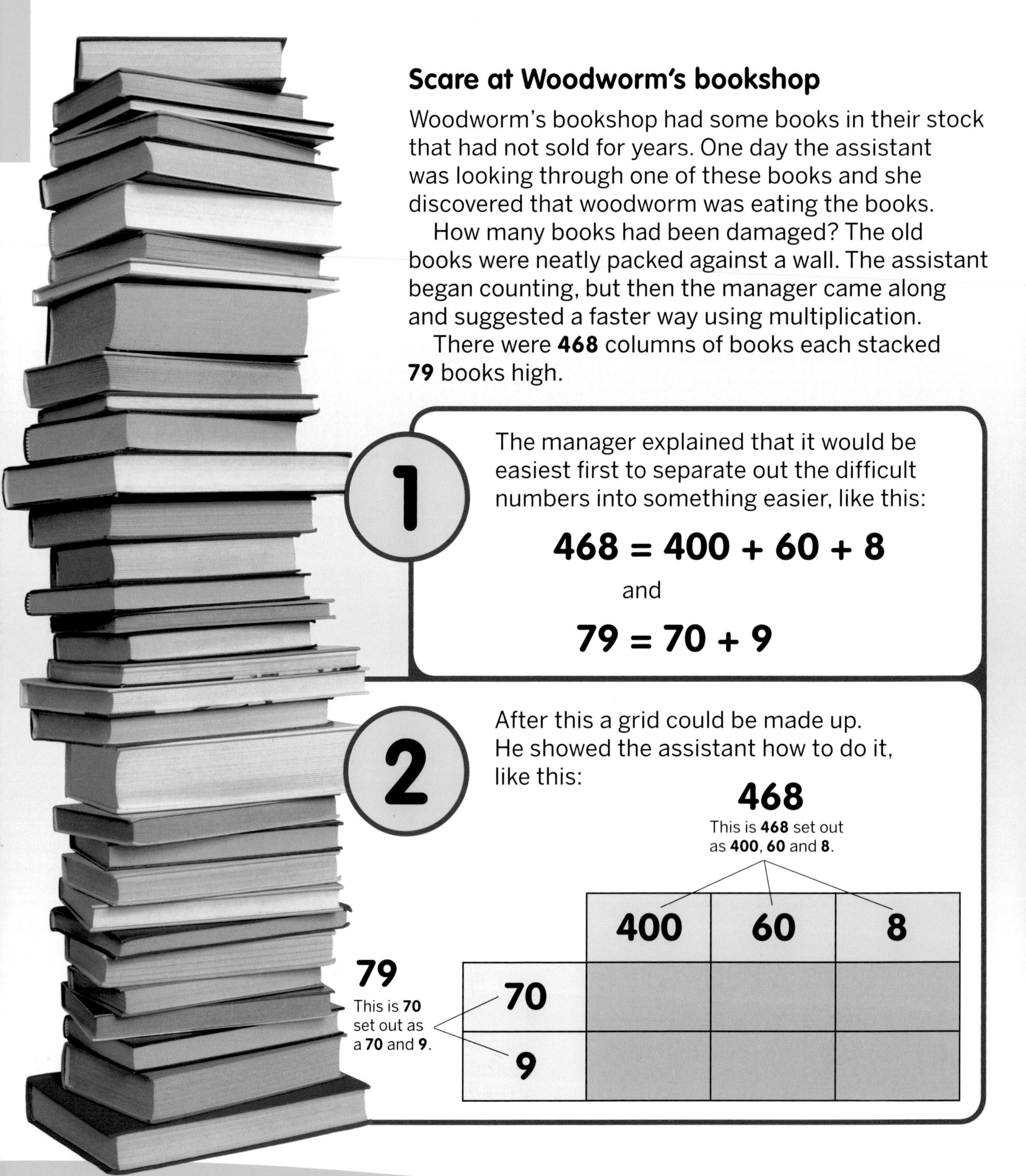

Scare at Woodworm's bookshop

Woodworm's bookshop had some books in their stock that had not sold for years. One day the assistant was looking through one of these books and she discovered that woodworm was eating the books.

How many books had been damaged? The old books were neatly packed against a wall. The assistant began counting, but then the manager came along and suggested a faster way using multiplication.

There were **468** columns of books each stacked **79** books high.

1

The manager explained that it would be easiest first to separate out the difficult numbers into something easier, like this:

$$468 = 400 + 60 + 8$$

and

$$79 = 70 + 9$$

2

After this a grid could be made up. He showed the assistant how to do it, like this:

468

This is **468** set out as **400**, **60** and **8**.

79

This is **70** set out as a **70** and **9**.

	400	60	8
70			
9			

3

He then filled in one of the squares for her, using the multiplication tables he had memorised (if you haven't memorised yours, then remember they are on page 17). In this case he used the fact that **8 × 7 = 56**, then remembered the number was **70**, not **7** and so added a **0** to his answer.

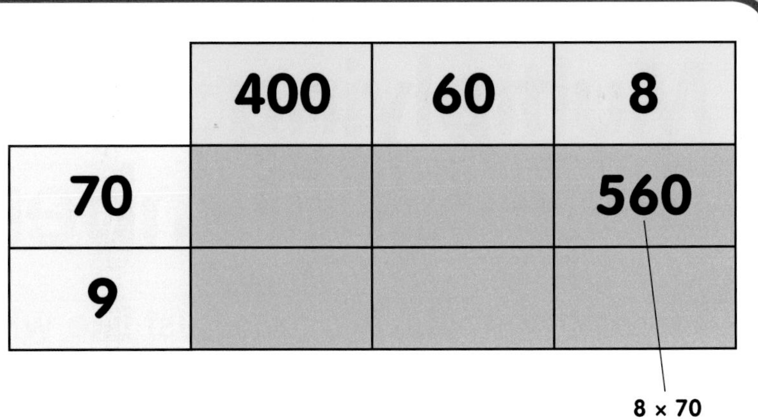

	400	60	8
70			560
9			

4

Here you can see all of the squares filled in. Check they are correct by using the multiplication square on page 15, or the tables on page 17.

	400	60	8
70	28,000	4,200	560
9	3,600	540	72

5

All the assistant had to do now was to add all the numbers in the squares. The addition is shown on the right.

The answer was **36,972**.

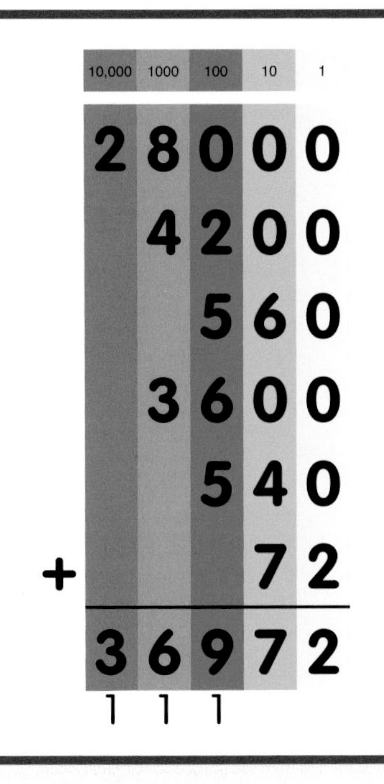

Can you do this?
Look back to page 21. How many days will you have been alive on your 28th birthday?

Hint: don't forget the leap years. (By the way, it will be the same day of the week as you were born on.)

Give your working out on a separate piece of paper.

Remember... How to multiply large numbers by using grids. Break the large numbers into simpler numbers, then complete the grid as shown here.

Multiplying decimal numbers

You can multiply decimals just like whole numbers. Just watch the decimal point!

Decimals show whole numbers and parts of numbers. A full stop is placed after the units, so that we will know which one it is. The full stop is called a decimal point.

Just as with whole numbers, which have the smallest on the right and the largest on the left, so every number to the right of the decimal point has a value ten times smaller than its left-hand neighbour. The further it is to the right, the smaller it is. Numbers below units are described as tenths, hundredths, thousandths and so on.

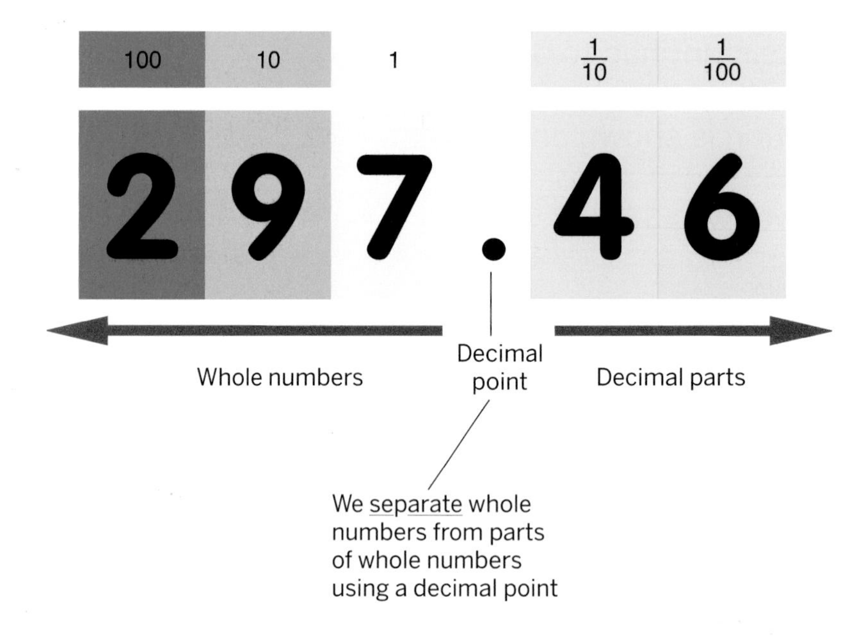

We separate whole numbers from parts of whole numbers using a decimal point

Remember... To multiply two numbers when one is a decimal, do the multiplication without the decimal point, then put the decimal point back in the answer, as many places from the right as it was in the original number.

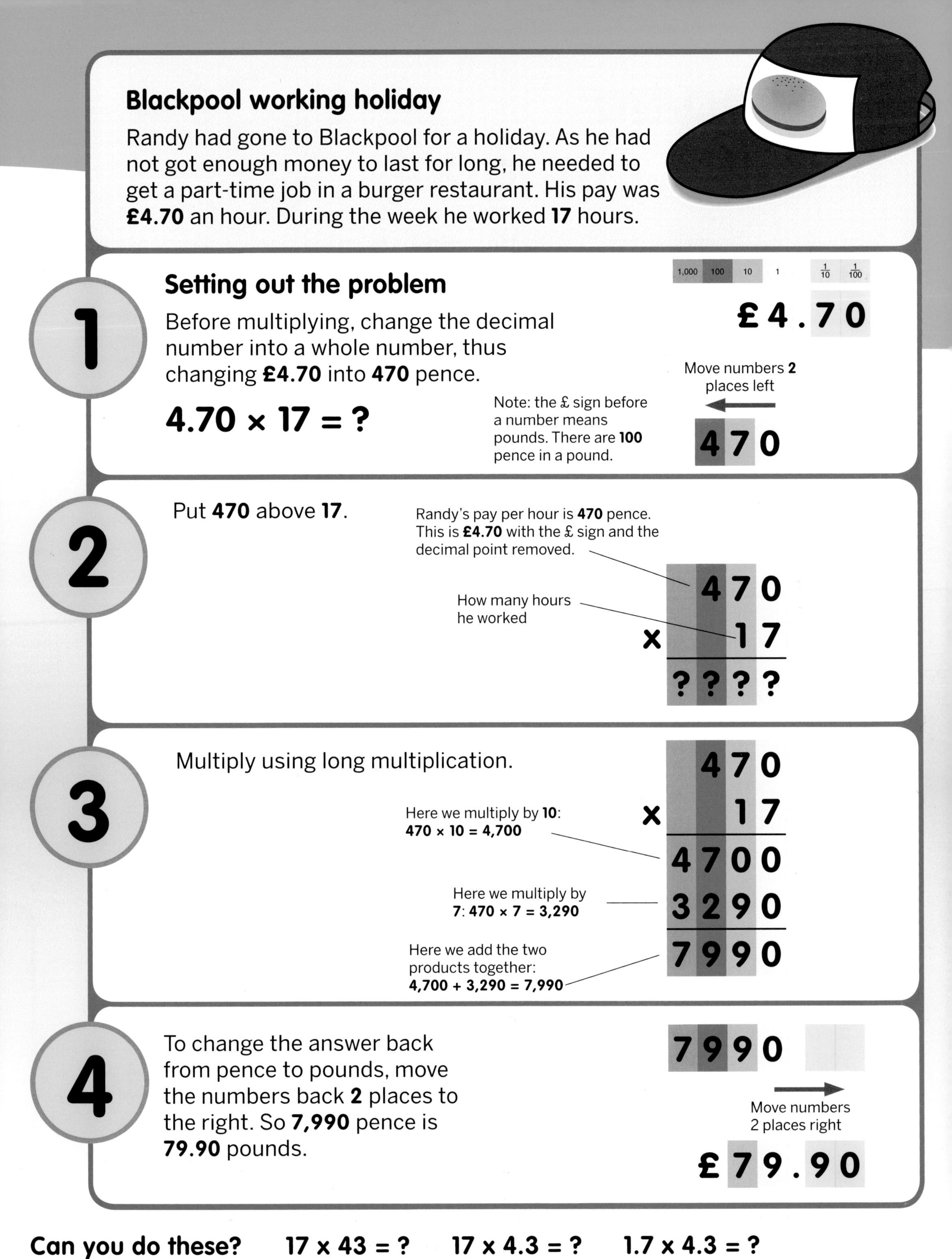

Blackpool working holiday

Randy had gone to Blackpool for a holiday. As he had not got enough money to last for long, he needed to get a part-time job in a burger restaurant. His pay was **£4.70** an hour. During the week he worked **17** hours.

1 Setting out the problem

Before multiplying, change the decimal number into a whole number, thus changing **£4.70** into **470** pence.

4.70 × 17 = ?

Note: the £ sign before a number means pounds. There are **100** pence in a pound.

2

Put **470** above **17**.

Randy's pay per hour is **470** pence. This is **£4.70** with the £ sign and the decimal point removed.

How many hours he worked

3

Multiply using long multiplication.

Here we multiply by **10**: **470 × 10 = 4,700**

Here we multiply by **7**: **470 × 7 = 3,290**

Here we add the two products together: **4,700 + 3,290 = 7,990**

4

To change the answer back from pence to pounds, move the numbers back **2** places to the right. So **7,990** pence is **79.90** pounds.

Can you do these? **17 x 43 = ?** **17 x 4.3 = ?** **1.7 x 4.3 = ?**

Work the answers out on a separate piece of paper.

Finding an unknown amount

Multiplying, together with adding, can help you find unknown amounts in an equation.

The duke's lost cuff link

It was a bad day in Wellington Castle. The Duke of Bute was in a temper because he had lost a diamond cuff link.

Then he had an idea. He marched off to the nearby village and told the children what had happened.

"Two years' pocket money, and ten gold pieces," said he, "to the sharp-eyed, nimble-fingered whippersnapper who can find my cuff link." Gold pieces were used as money in his country in those days.

There was no shortage of searchers! He marched back to the ducal bedroom, followed by an army of children. They swarmed everywhere: under the bed, behind the curtains, on top of the wardrobe, in the waste-paper basket, all through the bed covers – everywhere.

Finally Willi Wiesel squeaked: "Here it is!" The duke had dropped the cuff link inside a wellington boot. The duke was overjoyed, and gave Willi **34** gold pieces in a silk purse. However much do you think that duke supposed a year's pocket money was?

This is how we work it out

We have to write down how much the reward is in a number sentence:

'Two years' pocket money and ten gold pieces comes to **34** gold pieces'. Because we don't yet know what the duke thinks a year's pocket money is, we have to leave a space to work it out. We have used a **?** on the opposite page to show this unknown amount.

We can write the sentence again like this:

$$2 \times \boxed{?} + 10 = 34$$

We need to arrange for the **?** to be all on its own on the left-hand side of the equation.

First take **10** from both sides (remember if you do the same thing to both sides of an equation, you do not change the value of the equation).

The equation becomes:

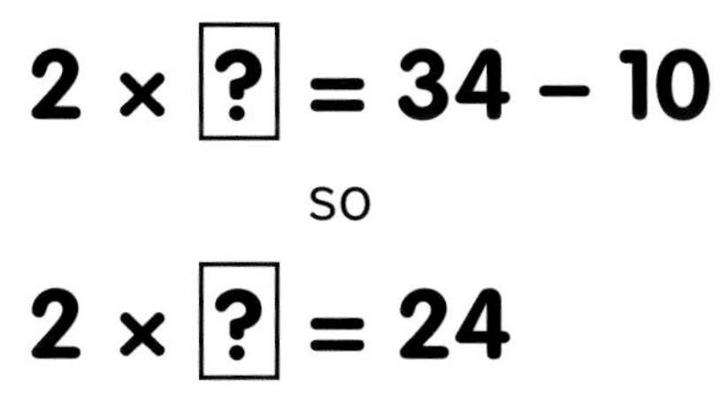

$$2 \times \boxed{?} = 34 - 10$$

so

$$2 \times \boxed{?} = 24$$

Now use the multiplication square backwards to find out which number times **2** produces **24**.

That gives:

$$\boxed{?} = 24 \div 2$$

$$\boxed{?} = 12$$

Now we know that the duke thought that a year's pocket money would be **12** gold pieces, or a gold piece a month.

Remember... This problem looked really hard, didn't it? But the answer was very simple. Remember, the first step is to convert words into an equation by putting a **?** for the unknown. Then you rearrange the equation to leave the **?** on its own.

Ludovici runs a health food store. His running costs are **£2,160** a week, made up of **£1,200** a week shop rent plus the wages of two assistants who each work five days a week.

Now that more people are buying health food, the store is really busy on Saturdays. How much extra profit would Ludovici have to make on a Saturday to pay for one extra Saturday assistant?

Running costs = rent + wages

or

$$2{,}160 = 1{,}200 + W$$

Wages = two assistants x five days x daily pay

or

$$W = 2 \times 5 \times P = 10 \times P$$

So our equation is:

$$2{,}160 = 1{,}200 + 10 \times P$$

Subtract **1,200** from each side of the equation:

$$960 = 10 \times P$$

As **96 x 10 = 960**:

$$96 = P$$

If Ludovici pays all the assistants the same, he must make an extra **£96** profit to pay the Saturday assistant's wages.

Can you do this? Replace **P** with **96** in **1,200 + 10 x P** to check that the answer is correct. Find **P** when **4 x P + 400 = 4,000**.

Give your working out on a separate piece of paper.

What symbols mean

Here is a list of the common maths symbols together with an example of how they are used.

$(8 + 9 - 3) \times \frac{2}{5} = 5.6$

+ The symbol for adding. We say it 'plus'. In Latin plus means 'more'.

− Between two numbers this symbol means 'subtract' or 'minus'. In front of one number it means the number is a minus number. In Latin minus means 'less'.

= The symbol for equals. We say it 'equals' or 'makes'. It comes from a Latin word meaning 'level' because weighing scales are level when the amounts on each side are equal.

( ) The symbols for brackets. You do everything inside the brackets first. Brackets always occur in pairs.

× The symbol for multiplying. We say it 'multiplied by' or 'times'.

—, **/** and **÷**
Three symbols for dividing. We say it 'divided by'. A pair of numbers above and below a **/** or **—** make a fraction, so **2/5** or $\frac{2}{5}$ is the fraction two-fifths.

• This is a decimal point. It is a dot written after the units when a number contains parts of a unit as well as whole numbers. This is the decimal number five point six.

Index